Forgotten Roots

Ștefan Dragoș Alexandru

ISBN: **978-973-0-29862-8**

This is for future me....

Cradle of Creation

12 December 2018

I see the most beautiful tree

With golden apples big as me

And I will climb this tree

To have a taste of LIFE that can be.

But now my eyes are open and see

The most vile, rotten and dark tree

It was always you and me

It was us humans who destroyed this tree.

Victims of Humanity

2

We sit and watch a beautiful rock

Tied skillfully to a red Dock

Sometimes it moves and now it sits

But from song it never quits.

- I once was a huge rock

But I became a fruit of mock

Every human made a run for it

And they tied, spit and smashed it.

Oceans nest

Feb. 24 2019

In the Ocean Deep

A clam was in deep sleep

But something disturbed her rest

And attacked her like a pest

It was so big yet steep

It was lost in the Voids Deep

It was the Immortal Guest

Death and plague were now in the Oceans nest.

A Broken Heart

25 Feb. 2019

A broken Heart was dancing

Not alone, but in a field of fallen flowers

And There were so many always

Trapped forever in a red Dance of Flowers

So sudden the dance is fading

And petals by the millions

All the way, smiling, crying, praying

Because the rest of them will dance again the dance of flowers.

Beauty and Greed

22 Feb. 2019

Since the dawn of time

I wanted to make you mine

And to tell you that all is fine.

A rainbow jumped into my eye

And made me feel like the dollar five

Now the lonely greedy fool is not fine.

Ode to a big Universe

26 Feb. 2019

So big yet dark

Like a long walk in the park

Planets, stars and all the rest

Worlds that forge the best.

And yet it is so very dark

How I want to switch on the Moon's arc

And make new worlds my nest

As I am the Universes guest.

Toughs of nothing

26 Feb. 2019

Shall the solid toughs of nothing

Be like drops of something

Jump on a wild idea

Much do about something into nothing

Just like snowing is to freezing

Another wild, wild ideea.

The Veil

27 Feb. 2019

A dark veil falls upon a young mind

Covering treasures on its path

And so the beautiful mind goes blind

Crying and trying to escape the veils wrath.

I do not want to be left behind

Alone after the veils bloodbath.

I want my mind to be unconfined

By age, health or times aftermath.

What once was

27 Feb. 2019

So much fog and ice and snow

But I guess we reap what we saw

With past days and forgotten hours

Our Eyes are full of sorrow

Do not yet sink so low

Free yourself and go with the flow

As we are just passing flowers

Floded by a rain of arrows in the Edge of tomorrow.

Have we forgotten?

3rd march 2019

The prints of time have made their mark

From here to then and then to Now

It seems like a walk in the park.

But you and I and I and me must know

What was then, now is just a big, black and dark

Did we truly forget what we saw?

... (We saw our end!)

The old man child

3rd march 2019

I crawl now and see

My mom and dad smiling back at me

I am happy as happy I can be.

I stand now but so alone

Because I have no home

My dad and mom now are gone.

I walk so slowly, still so alone

I survived the Drone

In tears of blood I cry alone.

My fear and I

3rd March 2019

Who is there and here forever?

Will I have you now or never?

Shall we be dammed together?

Can I have you until November?

I would put your face in ember

Just to see my fear forever.

One another

5 march 2019

Can I feel what I can see?

Or this is just all that it can be?

Will I be whatever?

Will I be whoever?

This is just a dream of me

I am trapped in a mind made by me

Can I be a regular old me?

Will that make me just another me?

Forsaken

Fractured dreams feel like broken glasses

I try, but seeing I cannot

I lost myself but my eyes are open

I twist my mind into a slipknot

How I want to be forsaken

What once was is forever, not.

Moving stars

Today I watch the universe dancing

And it is so mesmerizing

It is taking piece by piece

In a eternity of great place.

Atoms are forever moving

In a place of their own choosing

I am the one out of place

One small dot in Galaxies Game of Dice.

Mind Trap

5th March 2019

Today I find myself confused

Am I alive or am I a dream?

It is terrible but I am so amused.

In between realities my life is played

Here nobody can hear me scream

My life is just another record that many played.

Patriot

7th march 2019

Dance the patriot walk

Take a piece of chalk

And make your mark

On this Planet blue and dark.

Will you wake from this sleepwalk

Just to hear the last beat of the clock

Did the world promised you a park

No, it just kept you in the dark.

A man and his car

8th March 2019

Can your senses stretch so far?

Will you touch Nirvana with your car?

Don't be that man trapped in a tin van

Be that person that you can!

Mind Maze

8th March 2019

Damm I am trapped again

In my mind on a different plain

Can't go to see some more?

Won't I stay a little more?

These words leave me in great pain

Hopeless I try to win or gain at least a plane

Can't I go just some more?

Won't I live a little more?

Meaning of a World

My head is again hurting

So I hide my soul behind a curtain

No more pain let's do some healing

I will climb my logic with a feeling

The world is not a stain

But does that means it is annoying?

Dark Colors

9th March 2019

I see dark colors in the sky

But they don't bother you and I

One day the sky was clear and blue

When that was, I don't have a clue.

I always dreamed to fly

But how can I, in this black sky?

We tried to fix it with some glue

But now is too late for me and you.

What remains?

9th March 2019

Apples and oranges fall rotten from the tree

I am so hungry and I take a bite

How I miss when the air was free

In my mind a beautiful world I see

But then I take another bite

From a most vile and rotten tree.

In sickness

9th march 2019

In a world that became a lie

Children are born to die

The world is gone, O my my, my.

We made our bed and in it we must lie

Many of us open their eyes to die

History will sing for us and cry.

Hollow be thy spirit

11th March 2019

I hide beneath the shades of Darkness

I try to sleep on an empty mattress

Time is my only mistress

Falling down, again, the Rabbit hole into madness...

My souls friends is emptiness

I am a hollow lost in hate and bitterness

I hunger and shout in Hell's blindness

For souls to fill my eternal loneliness.

Human Pest

17 March 2019

All the birds are at their nest

All is good they need their rest

Can you be like all the rest?

Or you want to be the best?

Tonight you will be my guest

To a show that shows the rest

From Est to West

The World is eaten by the human pest.

Beasts of Pleasure

22 march 2019

In a Universe big and dark

We hear music from a park

And the Range is gone or Missing

Maybe He left for fishing.

Like one explorer named Clark

We went there to search this park

What we found was so intriguing

That we made another reading.

Disease was festering in the dark

Human soul was gone without a mark

Instead we found a great beast fighting

Looting, killing and some raping.

....

With one long blast we killed them all and planted others.

A game of faces

22 march 2019

Masks of burden lie in human flesh

Making memories feel so fresh

There, there put your face and smile

Like the rest of the human pile.

Tie those faces in a mesh

Can you feel the lie becoming fresh?

Make your face go the extra mile

And fool all of them with a smile.

Now you lost the game of faces

And your soul went to other places

What is, then the value of one soul

When you don't have a single goal?

Serpents tongue

22 march 2019

Maybe God created glory

Made all that is small and furry

But he created one like Him

One that was cast off by Him.

And we fall away, away

From a creator that did not seem to worry

Until a servant made by Him

Bite us until our light began to dim

Now we try to speak

But all is just a squeak

We are 8 billion but feel so weak

1000 tongues began to speak

And 8 billion began to freak

TO ALL THAT READ THESE PAGES...

I am Ștefan Dragoș Alexandru and I am from a small town from
Romania.
All that you just read are what I see and feel, the good with the bad and
the human mistake and misery with their ultimate demise.
What I treasure the most is our ability to seek more that our human
condition is currently offering for us.
As long as we continue to look on ways to improves ourselves we have a
chance to evolve and correct our mistakes, but when me stop all hope
will be lost.
Thank you for reading my small book and feel free to contact me or just
say hi. I can be found at YouTube: Cynetyc